D1508721

Paul's Call

Also by Kathleen Long Bostrom
From Westminster John Knox Press

Song of Creation

The Snake in the Grass
The Story of Adam and Eve

Green Plagues and Lamb
The Story of Moses and Pharaoh

Paul's Call

How Saul Became a Christian

Kathleen Long Bostrom

Illustrated by Dennis McKinsey

Westminster John Knox Press
LOUISVILLE • LONDON

© 2004 Kathleen Long Bostrom

All rights reserved. No part of this book may be reproduced or transmitted in any form or by any means, electronic or mechanical, including photocopying, recording, or by any information storage or retrieval system, without permission in writing from the publisher. For information, address Westminster John Knox Press, 100 Witherspoon Street, Louisville, Kentucky 40202-1396.

Book design by Teri Vinson
Cover design by Teri Vinson
Cover illustration by Dennis McKinsey

First edition
Published by Westminster John Knox Press
Louisville, Kentucky

This book is printed on acid-free paper that meets the American National Standards Institute Z39.48 standard. ♾

PRINTED IN HONG KONG

04 05 06 07 08 09 10 11 12 13 — 10 9 8 7 6 5 4 3 2 1

Library of Congress Cataloging-in-Publication Data

Bostrom, Kathleen Long.
  Paul's call : how Saul became a Christian / Kathleen Long Bostrom ; illustrated by Dennis McKinsey.— 1st ed.
    p. cm.
  ISBN 0-664-22636-1 (hard: alk. paper)
  1. Paul, the Apostle, Saint—Juvenile literature. I. McKinsey, Dennis. II. Title.

BS2605.5B67 2004
225.9'2—dc22
[B]
                                                                2003057678

*To the people of the First Presbyterian Church,
San Pedro, California—*

*You knew me when my name was "Long,"
And helped me in my search
To find my call to ministry,
My home within God's church.*

*With love and gratitude,
Kathy*

When the number of Christians
Was still very small,

One particular man
Did not like them *at all!*

Saul *hated* Christians! You could not appease him.
And if you ask why, I could guess at the reason.
It *could* be that Jesus was making the news.
It *could* be that Saul had a very short fuse.
Yet maybe the reason that has the best fit
Is that Saul simply didn't know Jesus one bit.

But,
Whatever the reason,
The news or the fuse,
Saul stood for the godly, defending the Jews.

He knew that the Christians were spreading the
   Word,
And he had to stop them before they were heard.

"They're saying that Jesus, who died on a cross,
Was King of the Jews, and the Son of the Boss!"
Then Saul growled, "I know where this whole
  mess is heading.
I must find some way to stop Christians from
  spreading."

For,
That Pharisee knew . . .
All the Christians believed in this whole Jesus
  craze.
They spent every moment just learning his ways.

And then! Oh, the praise! Oh, the praise! Praise!
  Praise! Praise!
That's what he most hated! The PRAISE!
  PRAISE! PRAISE! PRAISE!

And those Christians would gather,
All night and all day.
And they'd pray! And they'd pray!
And they'd PRAY!
         PRAY!
                  PRAY!
                           PRAY!

They would pray for their friends, and their
  enemies, too,
Which was something that Saul could not quite
  stand to do.

And THEN
They'd do something
That really irked Saul!
The thought of this thing made his skin start to
  crawl.

All the Christians took bread and a large cup of
  wine.
They'd sit 'round a table, those sickening swine.
They'd share! And they'd *share*!
And they'd share, share, share, SHARE!

They'd share until every last Christian was fed.
And the more that Saul thought of that wine
   and that bread,
The more he decided they all should be dead.
"Why, for all of my life I've put up with them now!
I MUST stop these Christians from spreading!
   . . . But HOW?"

Then Saul got a plan.
A horrible plan!
THAT SAUL
GOT A TERRIBLE, HORRIBLE PLAN!

"I'll go to Damascus! I'll put them to death!"
Saul uttered his threats with each miserable
  breath.
He made up his mind; it was all up to him.
The fate of those Christians was looking quite
  grim.

"All I need is permission . . .," he thought with a
  sneer.
"I'll go to the priest, who is not far from here."
And nothing could stop him, that crabby old
  beast.
He went, and he got the okay from the priest.

And then he wrote letters; he knew what to say:
"I'll stop everyone who is part of the Way."
And then he set out on that very same day.

THEN
He loaded a bag with a pile of letters.
He packed up the chains he'd be using for fetters.
He hardly could wait to begin the whole fracas.
So Saul headed off on the road to Damascus.

BUT then something happened he could not
  predict.
For one blazing moment Saul thought he'd been
  tricked.
A light flashed from heaven, so blindingly bright,
Saul fell to the ground with the loss of his sight.

And then came a voice, and poor Saul shook
  with fear.
The voice came from heaven; the message was
  clear.
It said quite explicitly, **"Saul, tell me why,
Why do you want to keep hurting me?
  WHY?"**

Then Saul said, "Who is this? Oh, who could
this be?"
The voice said, **"I'm Jesus; now listen to me.
I want you to go to the city, and wait.
And I will send someone to tell you your
fate."**

Saul got to his feet; he was blind and perplexed.
He went to Damascus to see what was next.

His friends dropped him off at a neighboring inn,
And left him alone, without kindred or kin.

For three days and nights, he did not eat or
  drink.
His mind was so stunned he could not even
  think.

THEN

God sent a man by the name Ananias,

A good-hearted Christian, quite faithful and
  pious.

God told him to go; it was really quite pressing:

The Pharisee, Saul, was in need of confessing.

And though this command was a little
   distressing,
The man, Ananias, with some second-guessing,
Did just what God asked him and gave Saul a
   blessing.

And what happened next? In the Bible they say
That a wonderful miracle happened that day.
When something like scales fell like rain from
  his eyes,
Poor Saul, he was taken by quite a surprise!

The Spirit of God reached down deep in his soul.
For the very first time in his life, he was whole.

And then, with his vision more keen than before,
Saul knew it was time he should settle the score.

He stayed in Damascus for several days,
And spoke about Jesus, and all were amazed.
Could *this* be the man who, a short time ago,
Was known as Jesus' mightiest foe?

Now, many were puzzled by Saul's sudden
  change.
They doubted his message and thought he was
  strange.
And Saul, it is true, really wasn't the same,
And with his new life, he received a new name.

His friends in the faith did not know him as *Saul*.
For the rest of his life,
they would all
        call
                Saul

                        PAUL.

Paul was on fire; his faith was so *hot!*
And then, as it happens more often than not,
The man who had fought against Christ with
    such force,
Began to preach Jesus until he was hoarse.

He preached in the churches. He preached to
  the Jews.
He preached to all people, of various views.
He preached, and he preached, and he shared
  the good news.
He preached to believers and those who had doubt.
Paul knew what it was he was preaching about.

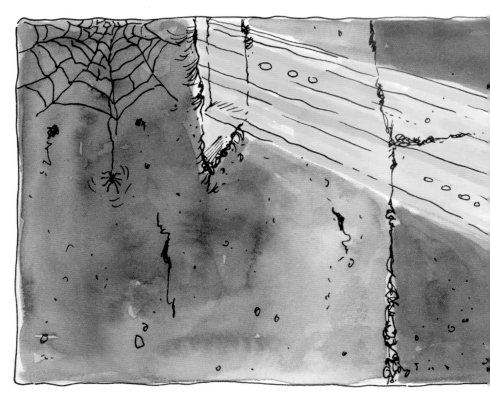

Paul gave every bit of his life to the Lord.
He gave and he gave, with no thought of reward.
Paul could not forget all the evil he'd done,
And those he had hurt for their faith in God's Son.

His life as a Christian was tragic and tough,
And though he was tortured and beaten and
  stuff,
Paul never believed he had given enough.
He did not have children, a home, or a wife.
Paul's steadfast conviction soon cost him his life.

When Paul got to heaven,
He found, by God's grace,
That Jesus had saved him
His own special place.

And Paul, who believed he was least of the
  least,
This Paul—he himself—was the guest at the
  feast.

God asks every person—
The large and the small,
The young and the old,
And the short and the tall—
To share the good news
So the world may discover

The way to love God
And to love one another.
You, too, have the chance
To be part of this story—
All praise be to Christ!
And to God be the glory!